Anacondas

Anacondas

Mary Ann McDonald

THE CHILD'S WORLD®, INC.

Library of Congress Cataloging-in-Publication Data
McDonald, Mary Ann.
Anacondas / by Mary Ann McDonald.
p.   cm.
Includes index.
Summary: Describes the physical characteristics,
behavior, habitat, and life cycle of the anaconda.
ISBN 1-56766-494-6 (lib. bdg. : alk paper)
1. Anaconda—Juvenile literature.
[1. Anaconda. 2. Snakes.]   I. Title.
QL666.063M36   1998
597.96—dc21   97-44645
CIP
AC

Photo Credits

© A.B. Sheldon: 24, 26
ANIMALS ANIMALS © A.J. Stevens: 29
ANIMALS ANIMALS © John Pointer: 6, 13
ANIMALS ANIMALS © Michael Dick: 20
ANIMALS ANIMALS © Partridge Productions Limited: 19
ANIMALS ANIMALS © Zig Leszczynski: 9
© 1998 Brian Kenney: 10, 15, 23, 30
© Joe McDonald: cover, 2, 16

On the cover...

Front cover: This *green anaconda* is very colorful.
Page 2: This *yellow anaconda* is sitting in the sunshine.

Table of Contents

Imagine that you are visiting the Amazon jungle. As your boat moves up a small river, you watch the shore carefully. Suddenly you see a snake lying on a branch hanging over the water. The snake is very large and thick and slightly green in color. As your boat moves closer, the snake drops into the water and quickly swims away. What was that huge snake? It was at least 15 feet long! Your tour guide called it a water boa—another name for an anaconda.

⇐ This green anaconda is moving down a tree.

Where Do Anacondas Live?

Anacondas live in the warm, tropical areas of South America, east of the Andes Mountains. They are found throughout Brazil's Amazon region and as far south as northern Argentina. They even live on the small island of Trinidad, north of Brazil.

Anacondas are **semi-aquatic**, which means that they spend some of their time in the water. They like to live near slow-moving rivers and swamps. They rest and sun themselves on branches that overhang the water. If something disturbs them, they simply drop into the water and swim away.

This yellow anaconda is waiting in the water for its next meal. ⇒

Anacondas, *boas*, and *pythons* all belong to the same animal family. This family contains the biggest snakes in the world. *Reticulated pythons* are the longest of all. They can be up to 33 feet long! Anacondas grow only to about 23 feet, but they are the heaviest snakes in the world. They can weigh 400 pounds and have a body 3 feet thick. The largest anaconda ever measured weighed 600 pounds. That's a big snake!

⇐ Green anacondas like this one can grow to be very large.

What Do Anacondas Look Like?

Anacondas don't have arms or legs like yours, but they do have some other familiar body parts. They have a heart, a stomach, a liver, kidneys, intestines, and lungs. All of these organs are long and slender so that they can fit inside the snake's body. Anacondas have many back bones, called **vertebrae**. These vertebrae make the snake flexible and strong. Large snakes can have up to 400 vertebrae! Like all snakes, anacondas developed from lizards a long time ago. In fact, anacondas still have two very primitive hind legs that look like small claws.

This anaconda is moving along in some short grasses. ⇒

What Color Are Anacondas?

Anacondas come in many shades of brown, green, and yellow. The largest kind of anaconda is sometimes called the *green anaconda* because of its olive and green colors. The smaller *yellow anaconda* has more yellow or golden tan.

All anacondas have dark spots or blotches all over their bodies. These patterns make the snakes harder to see. From above, anacondas look like sunlit spots on the water's surface. Anacondas are very well hidden from the animals they hunt for food. These animals are called their **prey**.

The spots on this yellow anaconda help it to hide. ⇒

Anacondas are **carnivores**, which means that they eat other animals. Young anacondas eat mostly fish. Adult snakes eat water birds, small animals, crocodiles, and even some larger animals. They occasionally will eat a dog, sheep, or pig.

Anacondas lie in shallow water near the shore, with only their eyes and nostrils above the water. They are very hard to see. When a prey animal comes to drink, the anaconda surprises it and kills it.

⇐ This yellow anaconda is waiting to surprise its prey.

How Do Anacondas Kill Their Prey?

Anacondas are **constrictors**, which means that they kill their prey by squeezing it to death, or "constricting." First the anaconda grabs its prey and holds it with its sharp, backward-curving teeth. Then the snake coils its body around the animal and begins to squeeze. Every time the animal takes a breath, the snake squeezes harder. Finally the animal stops breathing and dies.

This anaconda has killed a chicken by squeezing it. ⇒

Anacondas swallow their dinner whole. But how can the snake swallow something bigger than its own head? People once thought that anacondas crushed their victims' bones before swallowing, but that is not true. Instead, the anaconda opens its mouth wide enough to swallow the animal whole. How does it do that? By separating its lower jaw from the rest of its head! After it is done eating, the anaconda yawns widely to put its jaw back in place.

Do Anacondas Have Skin or Scales?

Anacondas have skin and scales. They look as if they are covered with scales, just like those of a fish. But a fish's scales are separate little pieces of skin. An anaconda's scales are just folds in its thick skin. Even the anaconda's eyes are covered with thin, clear scales called **spectacles**.

From close up, an anaconda's scales look very smooth. ⇒

An anaconda grows throughout its entire life. As it grows, it sheds its old skin whenever it outgrows it. First the snake knocks the old skin loose by rubbing its head against something rough. Then it hooks the loose skin on the rough object and crawls right out of its skin! The shed skin is inside out, but it matches the snake perfectly—right down to the spectacles.

Because they are so huge, anacondas do not move very quickly on land. They use special belly scales, called **scutes**, to move from one place to another. The scutes are larger than the other body scales and are in a single row. A strong muscle connects each scute to a rib. Anacondas dig their scutes into the ground and use them to push or pull their bodies along.

← This green anaconda is moving about by using its scutes.

How Are Baby Anacondas Born?

Anacondas give birth to live babies. The babies grow inside the mother within clear, soft eggs. There they stay safe and warm. Like a baby chicken, each baby anaconda feeds off the yolk of its egg. How many babies the mother has depends on her size. A large anaconda can give birth to over 50 babies, each about 3 feet long!

Once they are born, the young snakes quickly break free of their protective shells. They are on their own from the moment they are born. They must learn to hunt and to protect themselves without any help from their parents.

This newborn anaconda has just broken out of its clear egg. ⇒

Do Anacondas Make Good Pets?

Anacondas and other large snakes do not make good pets. Their size alone makes them a problem to keep and care for! Anacondas can also be very dangerous. Zookeepers never work alone around these snakes, which can easily kill an adult human. Anacondas are beautiful and interesting animals—but we are better off studying and appreciating them at a distance!

← Yellow anacondas like this one can be very dangerous.

Glossary

carnivores (KAR–nih–vorz)
Carnivores are animals that eat other animals. Anacondas are carnivores.

constrictors (kun–STRIK–turz)
Constrictors kill other animals by squeezing them to death. Anacondas and some other snakes are constrictors.

prey (PRAY)
Animals that are hunted and killed for food are called prey. Prey for anacondas includes fish, water birds, and other animals.

scutes (SKOOTS)
Scutes are large scales on an anaconda's belly. The scutes are attached to muscles and are used to push or pull the snake along.

semi-aquatic (seh–mee–ah–KWAH–tik)
Semi-aquatic animals live in the water some of the time. Anacondas are semi-aquatic.

spectacles (SPEK–tih–kullz)
Spectacles are clear scales that cover and protect a snake's eyes. Anacondas have spectacles.

vertebrae (VER–teh–bray)
Vertebrae are the bones that make up an animal's back. Big snakes like anacondas can have several hundred vertebrae.

Index